EDWARD

SNOWDEN

America's Whistleblower –

Sinner or Saint?

Phil Coleman

Table of Contents

Introduction

The revelation that Government organizations were spying on their own citizens, and those from other countries, shocked the world.

That this was probably legal, was even more astonishing.

In particular, the American NSA and British GCHQ, were intercepting communications – emails, phone calls, chat rooms, even normal internet usage – and monitoring them.

Not just the communications of those suspected of crime, or terrorists, but those of every single citizen.

They had been doing it for years.

The revelations came about because of one man. A young American with a great future came across the details of the Governments' actions, and decided to act.

Fearing for his freedom, even his life, he set up an elaborate programme of meetings with three trusted journalists.

These were reporters he knew would take him seriously, and would not be cowed by the enormity of what he had discovered.

With thousands of pieces of evidence, bordering on millions, this man revealed what he knew.

Edward Snowden.

Until 2013 completely unknown, but now one of the most notorious men on the planet.

He is viewed by some as a hero, a liberator, a spokesman for the people. A great patriot, who placed his nation above the petty interests of politicians seeking to create a platform for their own glory.

Regarded by many as heroic, brave, somebody prepared to stand up for what he believed.

By others as a traitor. A man who, through his actions, risked the lives of people all around the world.

A man who made it easier for terrorists to operate, for criminals to exist.

Whatever your view, it cannot be doubted that Edward Snowden, with his four laptops in tow, changed the world when, in 2013, he revealed his findings.

Revelations

Edward Snowden became a global news story in early June of 2013, just before his 30th birthday.

He released tens, maybe hundreds, of thousands of classified documents about the US Government to journalists Glenn Greenwald, Ewan MacAskill and Laura Poitras.

Also released was information about other nations, including Australia and Great Britain.

Whilst working for an agency servicing the NSA (the US's main surveillance group) he had come across information which caused him enormous alarm.

Four stories in particular where reported through the Guardian newspaper in Britain.

These were that Verizon, one of the America's major telecoms provider had been secretly ordered to hand over details of millions of calls to and from the USA.

Secondly, the cracking of internet encryption by the NSA and the British GCHQ.

Thirdly, that the US had been employing the surveillance of phone calls made by 35 world leaders.

And finally, revelations about the programme codenamed Prism.

We can look at each of these disclosures in turn.

The Verizon story caused special concerns because it highlighted that the collection of the calls was indiscriminate.

There was no prioritization towards those suspected of wrongdoing. The order granted by the Foreign Intelligence Surveillance Court covered a three-month period in 2013.

It meant that both location and the phone numbers of the speakers would be passed on to government officials. Whilst the content of the calls was not covered by the order, their time and duration were.

Snowden's leak was not the first in this area. Under Bush, even officials in security agencies had revealed the scale of official snooping.

However, Obama's regime was supposed to be marked by more openness and trust, but then these details were revealed under his leadership.

When the fact of the order was released, Verizon, White House officials and NSA staff all refused to comment. The order had stated that Verizon were not permitted to reveal what it had been made to do.

A fine legal definition was used to allow the order. Defined as 'metadata' rather than telecommunications, the order meant that there was no need to issue individual warrants for access to the communications.

Although the data requested did not include the names of the callers, it would be a simple matter to deduce this from the other information supplied.

The order, which was signed by Judge Roger Vinson, applied just to Verizon, but there could have been other orders applied to other providers. It would be odd to just limit the directive to one company.

When first set up, it was a mandate of the NSA that it would never use its surveillance systems in its home country. However, that lasted until just the mid-70s.

The explosion in home surveillance came during the post 9/11 period, under the Bush administration.

Back as far as the 1970s an investigation into the NSA's activities, conducted by Democrat Senator Frank Church warned against misuse of the organization's considerable powers.

The second revelation to find a rapid airing was the joint work by the NSA and its British counterpart, GCHQ (General Communications Headquarters) over the breaking of internet encryption codes.

This caused outrage to as significant a person as Tim Berners-Lee, who created the world wide web.

He is usually a mild-mannered man, not one you would expect as having changed the way the majority of the world now lives. But his response to the work of the NSA and GCHQ was substantial.

'I think it's appalling' he told the Guardian newspaper.

The story was jointly released with The New York Times and ProPublica, an investigative newsroom.

The internet genius felt that exposing the encryption processes would open up opportunities for exploitation by those acting for their own, or negative, interests.

He argued that the British and American agencies had opted for the lowest of common denominators, behaving in the same way as those they claim to watch.

He also believes that the web is for everyone, not something to be controlled and monitored by Governments.

Indeed, during the 2012 London Olympics' opening ceremony, he appeared during Danny Boyle's extravaganza typing the words 'This is for everyone' on a computer screen.

Somewhat ironic, that, given the wide support the British Government offered to make those Olympics a success.

Whilst he accepts that the legality of what the agencies did might be hard to disprove, he questions their ethics.

FISA (the foreign intelligence surveillance act) is widely seen as unaccountable, and GCHQ deeply secretive.

Recognizing that, despite the morally high expectations of web usage, sometimes people, groups and nations do fall short, security does have to be maintained.

However, he thinks that such security must be with the support and knowledge of the public, and not be imposed behind their backs.

The surveillance of phone calls and other communications of world leaders is probably the most embarrassing to the US of Snowden's revelations.

Amongst such a wealth of data, it is hard to be precise how many of these heads of government were monitored, with there being strong evidence of at least 35, and indications that this number could be as high as 122.

The list includes Abdullah Badawi, a former Prime Minister of Malaysia and a previous Ukrainian Premier, Yulia Tymoshenko.

However, it is the information that German Chancellor Angela Merkel was on the list that caused most embarrassment.

Not only were her communications being monitored, but her mobile phone usage had been watched for up to ten years.

Germany, before the Berlin Wall collapsed, had of course existed in a permanent state of tension, with the Communist state of East Germany next door.

Its secret police were the feared Stasi, and Merkel compared the US's action to theirs. Hardly good PR for the Americans to be seen as spying on one of their main allies.

Further than this, GCHQ had also become involved in the infiltration of the servers run by German internet companies.

The final revelation of the big four group amongst the many stories unearthed by Snowden's actions concerned the programme, Prism.

The programme enabled the collection of communications on fiber cables and infrastructure as data flowed between its source and destination.

It took information from a number of major US Service Providers, including Google, Facebook, Microsoft, Yahoo, Pal Talk, Apple, YouTube, AOL and Skype.

In fact, close to all the online communications platforms most Americans would use.

The programme gave the NSA access to pretty much every element of online activity, and that includes online chat and emails.

Once again, the programme started under the Bush Administration, but it was renewed, secretly, under Obama. It is also believed that it was done without the knowledge of the providers.

And, because the main internet companies tend to be based in the US, it means that the Government there had access to every single communication sent from anywhere in the world.

In theory at least, although quite how it would manage such a magnitude of data is hard to understand.

Rather like each of the other revelations, the legality of Prism was open to question. It is hard to see how the US could have access to, say, an email sent from the UK, but the programme exploited the fuzziness around such international laws.

The British equivalent to Prism, Tempora, was created under the twin titles of 'Mastering the Internet' and 'Global Telecoms Exploitation'.

This allowed GCHQ to look into anybody's web usage, emails, phone calls and social media entries.

Snowden claimed that the UK exploitation was even greater than that of the US.

And, with getting on for a million US citizens involved directly or indirectly with the NSA, a huge number had access to British communications.

The relationship between GCHQ and some of the commercial companies from whom they were able to extract data involved some degree of payment.

In return for which, their anonymity was ensured. Mind you, should they take a moral high ground and refuse to co-operate, the law is such that they could be compelled to do so.

However, a spokesman at the time said that the focus of the GCHQ searches was towards economic well-being, organized crime and terrorism.

It seems as though the operation is legal, although only through the twisting of laws which allow data collection of communications heading abroad.

Such is the nature of the web that much information does this before it is returned to the UK.

However, when the law GCHQ relies upon was established, towards the turn of the millennium, there was no inkling of how it may be subsequently used.

The interceptions are claimed to have led to the prevention of a number of terrorist attacks, including some at the Olympics.

But, Snowden would ask, what price has been paid for that security?

The Journalists

Although he wrote widely on security issues, Glenn Greenwald had never considered the need for an encryption key for the stories that were fed to him daily.

For a journalist in his position, with his reputation as a fearless exposer of Government wrongdoing, he knew that many of the emails he received were untrue.

They were often sent by cranks and madmen, the kind who felt that the CIA was hunting them down.

But amongst the nonsense would be the occasional gem.

One such diamond was received on December 1st, 2012. Greenwald opened his inbox to find a message asking for his public encryption key, so an email could be sent securely.

Indeed, as Greenwald had expressed support for WikiLeaks and Bradley Manning, it was likely that he was already on the US Government's watch list.

But Greenwald was a busy man, and chose to ignore the request. The source, though, did not give up, and next sent details of how to set up an encryption key.

But still he did not feel that the matter was demanding enough of his attention. The source needed to capture Greenwald's interest to get him to set up the security system.

But he would not do so until the security system was in place to offer protection. A classic Catch 22 scenario.

That was that. But sixth months later, a documentary maker, Laura Poitras, contacted him. The two were friends, and Greenwald listened to her story.

When the two journalists and their source met, in Hong Kong seven months after the initial contact, the writers would be presented by what the CIA called:

'The most serious compromise of classified information in the history of the U.S. intelligence community.'

But why had Snowden contacted Greenwald in the first place? His main work was for a British, rather than American, newspaper.

The Guardian, based in London, was best known for its typo errors, and was nicknamed the Grauniad (invented by the satirical magazine Private Eye).

A serious paper, it typically supported left of center ideas, although was very much a mainstream periodical.

However, Snowden had learned that the New York Times had sat on a similar Government revelation to some of those he held, and he wanted an outlet that would publish.

Greenwald had such a reputation. He was a hero of liberty seekers, with a left-wing political viewpoint.

He was a former lawyer who had been a staunch defender of victims of civil liberty breaches.

He is notoriously up for the fight – colleagues quote that he 'lives to piss people off' and he had challenged the full range of what was becoming mainstream politics.

His targets included the Tea Party, both Republicans and Democrats, Obama and Bush plus, on top everything else, Congress.

Greenwald held a particular dislike of faux liberal journalists, whom he accused of cozying up to Governments, giving them the freedom to act as they wished under a blanket of false openness.

He also felt that political thinkers with influence were part of a closed club, and needed to be challenged to move them on from their self-satisfied demeanors.

His anti-establishment, anti-status quo position had earned Greenwald a large following of those of a similar viewpoint, particularly young idealists.

Snowden was a member of that group. It was believed that Greenwald would reveal truths, no matter what the consequences.

Greenwald has been based in Brazil for many years, where he lives in comfort with his partner, David Miranda and a large collection of adoring dogs.

He moved to Lauderdale Lakes, Florida, after leaving Queens when still young. His home was typically working class of the time.

His mother worked all kinds of jobs,
including taking the money *cashiering* at a local
Macdonald's to support him and his brother.

His political viewpoints were influenced and formed under the admiration he held for his grandfather.

Louis Greenwald was a councilman who battled hard on behalf of the poor in his community.

Glenn took to politics from a young age, running for council office whilst still in High School.

He later said that his grandfather had taught him that there was nothing more important and noble than to stand up for those marginalized in society.

Being a young, gay teen in 1980s America meant that he very much fitted that category.

His determination to be honest to his character when to be homosexual was still considered akin to carrying some horrible disease led him into conflict right from the start.

He challenged his teachers constantly, picking up on unreasonable rules and regulations. His love of argument led him to becoming a debating star and state champion, and he went on to University.

After a spell with a corporate law form, he set up his own practice so that he could . follow his beliefs more fully.

He once spent years defending the rights of neo Nazis to express their views, as odious as he found their beliefs.

Indeed, in another example of the inherent contradictions he sought to exploit, he became a regular on serious broadcasts.

But whilst his well-evidenced rhetoric was anti-establishment, he ensured a very conservative appearance. Wearing suit and tie, he would come across as distinctly 'one of us' in everything but his words.

In the post 9/11 period, when such was the patriotism (or jingoism, if you prefer) that it seemed as if the Government had free reign to do as they pleased, Greenwald became especially riled.

The case of Jose Padilla was a matter in point, Greenwald felt outraged that the bomber could be arrested, initially denied access to representation, and held for years without charge.

It seemed as though the line in the sand had been erased.

In 2005 he took off for a lengthy holiday in Brazil, and met Miranda. He moved there within a year and began a successful career as a blogger.

Just as how Snowden would later feel, he was enraged when he discovered that the New York Times had sat on a politically sensitive news story.

Two of the paper's investigative journalists, James Risen and Eric Lichtblau, had discovered that the Bush administration had authorized the NSA to run a programme allowing it to tap whomever it wished.

However, the Bush office pressured the paper not to reveal the story, and it caved in. Greenwald felt this to be a complete betrayal of journalistic duty and honor.

The seeds of partnership between Snowden and Greenwald were sewn.

But, as stated earlier, they would not have come to fruition without the input of Laura Poitras.

They had met up, along with Guardian journalist Ewen MacAskill, at JFK Airport, where the documentary maker showed Greenwald more of the leaked documents.

It was a goldmine of secrets. The seeds had begun to germinate, and soon they would bloom.

Poitras was already under watch. She had produced the film, My Country, My Country, in 2006. The film examined the treatment of Iraqi nationals in their homeland under US occupation.

The film was nominated for an Oscar, but led to her being stopped and detained on tens of occasions at US borders.

The US has a record of this sort of behavior. In 2017, the cameraman behind a film examining UN behavior in Syria – White Helmets – was refused entry, not even being allowed to get on the plane he was taking from Istanbul.

In fact, Poitras later took further action to find the reason behind the obstructions she faced, and was ultimately told, following her filing of a lawsuit. It was because she had information about an atrocity carried out on US troops.

She completely denies this.

She had learned inscription to keep her stories private from snoopers.

Later, she would be even more successful with her film about Snowden, Citizenfour, which was victorious in the category of Best Documentary Feature at the Oscars.

Prior to that, she won the George Polk Award for national security reporting for work on the NSA disclosures.

The award is designed to celebrate excellence in journalism, both print and broadcast.

She was also a part of the group of four – Greenwald and MacAskill, plus Washington Post reporter Barton Gellman – who won the 2014 Pullitzer Prize for Public Service.

She followed this by working for a time with the German magazine Der Spiegel exposing the NSA surveillance taking place in Germany.

Along with Greenwald and another journalist (Jeremy Scahill) she formed a media outlet sponsored by Ebay founder Pierre Omidyar.

This was established with the aim of addressing concerns about the freedom of the press, both in the US and around the world.

Poitras, who was born in 1964, grew up in Boston to wealthy parents, from whom she inherits a sense of public duty. Her parent donated $20 million in 2007 for research into brain disorders.

Following a period working as a chef, she took her interest in filmmaking further, and graduated in this discipline in 1996.

The third of the three journalists initially involved with Snowden is Ewen MacAskill.

At the time Snowden began to reveal his findings, MacAskill was chief Washington DC correspondent for the Guardian.

His role in the initial interviews was to be the Guardian's representative – at the time the revelations began, he thought that he was hearing the biggest story of the week.

'Decade' might have been a better description.

MacAskill was born in Glasgow in the early 1950s, and took up senior roles at The Scotsman newspaper in the 1990s. After his work with Snowden, for which he was cited in the Pullitzer Prize award, he moved on to become the Guardian's chief security correspondent.

One additional reporter would also play a significant role in the stories. Although not involved at the outset, Barton Gellman became the other person entrusted to share the secrets.

Gellman worked for the Washington Post. A paper with, of course, a strong reputation for spilling the beans on political wrong-doing. (If that is your view on the NSA's activities.)

Back in 1972, two of its reporters had exposed President Nixon and the Watergate Scandal. Watergate itself was a Washington Office block which had been burgled.

The block housed some Democratic Party offices.

Carl Bernstein and Bob Woodward were the reporters working on the story. With the help of a notorious source – Deep Throat – it became apparent that Nixon himself was implicated.

Deep Throat (a senior official at the FBI, Mark Felt) was able to point the journalists in the right direction with their investigations.

It ultimately came out that the break-in was part of a series of irregularities employed to support Nixon's re-election campaign.

There is no suggestion that either Bush or Obama had anything to gain from the NSA actions – in fact, they probably had more to lose.

However, the Post's reputation as a hard-hitting political observer was enhanced.

Gellman himself came to prominence following his eyewitness reports on the attacks on the World Trade Centre in 2001.

He followed this by closely reporting on the war with Al Qaeda. Prior to the Twin

Towers attacks he had followed both Clinton and Bush's 'War on Terror'.

In particular, he had reported on the misuse of intelligence regarding weapons of mass destruction.

These caused him to fall into poor relations with the CIA. Later, following revelations about abuse of powers marauding under the Patriot Act, the Justice Department shared the CIA's displeasure.

Although he had left the Post to concentrate on his own book writing, he was rehired when the Snowden revelations became known.

He spent some time with Snowden in Russia, and hinted that there were even bigger stories to reveal.

Apart from Poitras and Glennwald, he is the only person to have seen the full set of Snowden papers.

Growing Up

Edward Snowden had a relatively unexceptional early life, with few indications that he would one day become perhaps the most famous political dissident on the planet.

Snowdon was born into a comfortable, middle class background, with a strong history of official service in the family.

His grandfather, on his mother's side, worked for the FBI and was one of those at the Pentagon when the building was attacked on September 11th. This was in the year that Edward Snowden's parents divorced.

Snowden's mother, Elizabeth, is chief deputy at the US District Court in Maryland, and his father (Lonnie) was an officer with the coast guard.

Even his sister, Jessica, worked as a lawyer with the Federal Judiciary in Washington DC.

With such strong family ties it might be seen as inevitable that you Edward would one day follow in the family footsteps of government service.

He was an extremely bright boy, scoring 145 in IQ tests, but for all of his ability, he found school difficult.

When the family moved to Maryland from his place of birth, Elizabeth City North Carolina, he missed nearly a year of schooling, and from that point he was an irregular attender.

Perhaps like many super intelligent children he found the restrictions of a formal education frustrating and limiting.

He took his own GED test, to demonstrate that he had the skills of a High School student. These tests are normally seen as a 'second opportunity' route for High School dropouts.

From there, he enrolled in the Anne Arundel Community College in Maryland to further his education.

He did not take an undergraduate degree, but worked online at Liverpool University pursuing a Masters.

As a young man, he developed an interest in Japanese culture, learning the language and working for an anime company which had an office in the US.

He was also fascinated by Mandarin, and became involved in martial arts.

These are not especially unusual activities and interests for a very bright young man in his late teens.

However, when he turned twenty he enlisted in the US army. Here was another indication that Snowden was not just any man.

He was disappointed that there was no option for a person to declare themselves agnostic on the enlistment form, and chose to call himself a Buddhist instead.

Soon he attempted to join the special forces team. He spent five months waiting to begin training, but was subsequently refused entry to the programme.

The reason why is kept secret.

He had attempted to join the army because he had wanted to fight in the Iraq War. This was because he felt it was an obligation, as a member of the human race, to free people from oppression.

Such a high moral stance might have been a driving force behind his decision to reveal the NSA secrets a few years later.

Snowden's military experiences ended when he broke both legs in a training accident.

His political viewpoints are complex. Clearly not a fan of George Bush, nevertheless he did not either vote for Obama in the 2008 election, nor John

McCain, apparently opting for one of the alternative candidates.

He was prepared to give Obama a chance to repair some of the damage he believed Bush had perpetrated but quickly became disillusioned.

He especially disliked the appointment of Leon Panetta to run the CIA, feeling that the man was a politician rather than a specialist, and was therefore in place for purely political reasons.

Logic would deduce that a man with such feelings against state snooping would lie on the left of political leanings, but this does not seem to have been the case with Snowden.

He was against the principle of social security, although felt all were entitled to enough money to live on, whatever their circumstances.

He was fiercely opposed to restrictions on gun ownership and believed in a return to the gold standard.

He was a fervent supporter of internet freedom, and his laptop displayed stickers for ~~two of these~~ the Tor Project and Electric Frontier Foundation.

After recovery from his training accident, he spent a year working as a security specialist at the University of Maryland.

Employing his skills with languages, he worked in their centre for the Advanced Study of Language.

Although the centre was sponsored by the NSA it was not classified, but was heavily guarded. Apparently, he had needed to take a polygraph test and pass a high level security assessment to work there.

His interest in intelligence services spiked; he attended a job fair focusing on this career path and was appointed to a position at the CIA.

His love of all things technical served him well, and he made rapid progress, quickly being sent to a secret institution which specialized in technology.

He lived in a hotel for six months whilst completing this course.

By 2007 he was being moved abroad. Snowden became responsible for computer security and network safety in Geneva, Switzerland.

He was assigned to the US contribution to the United Nations. He received an expensive four bedroomed apartment overlooking Lake Geneva and a diplomatic passport whilst working in the country.

Such was his burgeoning reputation, that Snowden was selected to support the president at the 2008 Nato summit in Rome.

However, he was also beginning to lose some of the idealism of youth. An incident occurred which Snowden describes, but which is disputed by the Swiss authorities.

On one occasion, allegedly, the CIA got a Swiss banker drunk, then encouraged him to drive his car home.

He was arrested, perhaps because of a tip off, but the CIA offered to support him in exchange for him becoming an informant.

Snowden left the CIA in 2009.

The NSA is a major employer in the United States. It has around 40000 employees, but it also sub contracts thousands more.

In effect, there is little difference – once work has been allocated – between being a sub-contractor or a full employee.

One of the companies from whom the NSA sub contracted in 2009 was Dell. This technological giant managed tech systems for a whole range of Government departments.

Snowden moved to Dell after he left the CIA. His first task was to support officials – civil and military – as they sought to protect their systems from Chinese hackers.

As with the CIA, he moved quickly through the ranks, progressing from the role of a supervisor to becoming identified as an expert in cyber counterintelligence.

In 2011 he returned to Maryland, where he worked closely with senior CIA officials working in their technical fields.

From there, in early 2012, he was posted to Hawaii, to work specifically for the NSA, operating as their lead technologist for their information sharing office.

It was during this role that he began to identify concerns in the operations of the NSA, and started to download and copy the information for which he would shortly become famous.

Snowden had fallen in love whilst living in Hawaii. With an enormous salary – in excess of $200000 – and a beautiful young girlfriend, he had a lot to lose by telling his story.

Lindsay Mills was a dancer when she met Snowden. The two had even reached the point of considering marriage when both of their lives changed.

Snowden had not told his pole dance loving girlfriend about his plans, nor the secrets he had discovered, most probably to protect her from the scrutiny that would follow.

She was devastated when he left, but some reports show her spending time in Moscow –

Snowden moved to seek asylum in Russia - and the documentary Citizenfour indicated that the couple still spent time together.

But such is the secrecy surrounding Snowden since his revelations, that the public cannot be sure.

Discovering the secrets

Despite the seniority of his role, Snowden would still have found accessing and then downloading the NSA revelations difficult, as well as life-threateningly risky.

He may have had, knowingly or not, help from colleagues, but Snowden has displayed throughout the time since he first leaked the reports a strong wish to protect others.

Snowden describes seeing the Director of National Intelligence, James Clapper, lying to Congress – whilst under oath – as the straw that broke the camel's back.

He left Dell and took a pay cut to join another firm linked to security, Booz Allen.

Whilst working there, he was also organizing the millions of files of data he had downloaded.

He had not taken on security work with the intention of exposing secrets, but concerns had begun to grow.

He had witnessed young programmers having access to endless sources on information about citizens. He describes occasions where the young workers would come across compromising photos.

They would share them with colleagues, for a laugh, but before long that person's whole life would have been scrutinized, simply because it could be.

He felt that such behavior was unacceptable. Most of us would agree.

Although the NSA deny it, he claims to have reported his concerns on more than one occasion, but had been ignored.

Some senior colleagues supported his views, but they were afraid to say too much – the NSA seemed to have a very intolerant approach to whistle blowing.

The organization did recognize, however, that they had a jewel in Snowden and had offered him promotions to extremely senior roles.

But by this time, he was disillusioned – more – he recognized what he saw as significant wrong doing in the organization. From the top. He turned down these promotions.

Following the revelations, the NSA and Government agencies went into hurricane force spinning mode, trying to discredit their former star.

It was alleged that he had tricked colleagues into revealing passwords and access codes using which he accessed restricted files.

He has always denied doing so. Whatever, Snowden polarized opinion.

Hero or villain?

To the hard line hawks of American politics and society, he is no more than a traitor who has placed the lives of many at risk.

To the liberals, he is a brave hero who has risked all to reveal the truth.

But how do most of the public regard him in the US?   Also in Britain – he revealed many details about the actions of GCHQ? In fact, how does the world see him?

And, just as importantly, what were his own motivations for the actions he took? We have seen in the previous chapter that Snowden became disillusioned.

We know that he held strong views. He joined an on line technology discussion site, operating under a pseudonym. The views he expressed were clear, and strong.

He hated interventions into internet freedom.

But we have also seen that, apart from a ~~not~~ untypical young person's distrust of the established political parties, his views fitted under a mainstream heading.

It would be fair to judge that Snowden's stated belief – backed up by Glenn Greenwald – that he felt the NSA were going too far and exceeding their ~~remit~~ limit was genuine.

And he felt that people needed to know.

Snowden received wide acclaim for his whistleblowing. Having revealed his knowledge to the Guardian newspaper, he was the overwhelming winner of their Person of the Year 2013.

The Foreign Policy institute placed him first in their list of Global Thinkers, also in 2013. This was purely based on his revelations.

In analyzing his impact on global news that year, the organization found that only President Obama – and that by just a little – had generated more interest.

The Times placed him as second in their Person of the Year award in the year of his releases. Only the Pope came higher.

With stories still regularly appearing, he remained in their list of the top one hundred most influential people in the world in 2014 as well.

TechRepublic placed him as the top Tech Heroes of 2013. The online newspaper, which is read by IT professionals, identified his role in revealing the implications of the NSA actions for those working in the field of technology.

He was invited to join the board of directors of the Freedom of the Press Association in 2014. Glenn Greenwald and Laura Poitras are also on this committee.

And, he was made an honorary member of the Freie University in Berlin in recognition of his achievements in defending 'transparency, justice and freedom.'

On top of mention in so many media list, he also earned several awards.

Although in hiding at the time, he was awarded the German Whistleblower Prize. This award, which is presented every other year, recognizes the bravery and intentions of whistleblowers internationally.

He was awarded this in recognition of his efforts to expose the unforeseen scale of monitoring and storage of data by Government agencies.

When he was awarded the Sam Adams Award in October 2013, Snowden made his first public appearance for two months to accept it.

The recognition is made annually and is awarded to an intelligence professional who has taken a stand on behalf of integrity and ethics.

Sam Adams was a CIA officer who discovered that the army was underestimating the number of Vietcong and North Vietnamese soldiers during the Vietnam war.

He faced long term persecution for his whistleblowing.

So, not much change there for Snowden.

The award takes the form of a candlestick, but is considered high recognition indeed for a person who has stood up for their beliefs.

It was presented to him by another whistleblower, Jesselyn Radack, who had been an FBI officer.

He said that, despite the anger and poison that was coming from the Government and much of the media back in the States, public opinion was very much in support of Snowden's actions.

At Christmas in Britain, the Queen delivers a traditional speech to the people. Usually screened after lunch, many tune in to hear her words.

Channel Four is a mainstream broadcaster but one that often delivers alternative programming. It publishes an alternative Christmas Day message.

In 2013, Laura Poitras produced this speech, in which Snowden compared Government surveillance with that imagined in George Orwell's novel, 1984.

In this, Big Brother not only patrols what its citizens say, but also what they believe and think. The thought police are omnipresent.

Offenders are sent to Room 101, a torture chamber in which they are confronted by their worst fears.

If the internet – thought at the time to be relatively private – was a medium through which people could express their views, whatever they might be, then the monitoring of that made the comparison more than reasonable.

Germany holds its own Big Brother awards, an anti-intrusion occasion. But in 2014, it created a new title, the first 'positive' award.

Called the Julia and Winston Award (named after the heroic protagonists in the Orwell novel) it took the form of a million free stickers which encouraged the German Government to give asylum to Snowden.

As angry as the Germans were for the surveillance intrusion into their Chancellor, it seems as though economic and political relations with the mighty market place that in is the US were more important.

Asylum was not offered.

Poitras was again linked with Snowden in their joint receipt of Ridenhour Truth-Telling Prize.

Snowden appeared by video link to accept the award, and took part in a question and answer session with the audience.

Standing ovation followed standing ovation, and during the occasion – which honors whistleblowers and those promoting transparency in public life – and these prompted a rhetorical question from the man of the moment.

He wondered why the US Government had swiftly charged him, when James Clapper – he of the infamous lie to Congress – had never even been reprimanded?

The Swedish foundation, Right Livelihood, gave an honorary award to Snowden, along with the Guardian editor, at the end of 2014.

Snowden's bravery was widely respected by the young, and in 2014 the student body of Glasgow University appointed him to the honorary role of Rector.

The position runs for three years, and whilst it is ceremonial, nevertheless Snowden's exile meant that he was never able to visit the University.

And still the list continues. But it is important to see the scale of the support Snowden received from significant bodies, especially those who support the promotion of civil liberties.

There are many who feel that numerous Governments, including those in the US and Britain, are seeking to use the rise of terrorism as a front snoop into the lives of their populace.

It is an easy excuse to use for looking into people's lives, and to make judgements about which views and actions are deemed unacceptable to the elected – and unelected – leaders.

The McCarthy witch hunts received enormous criticism at the time and later, and

Governments learned to be more secret in their invasion into people's lives.

The British war hero and decoder Alan Turing is widely accepted as one of the most significant contributors to the allies' victory in World War II.

By decoding the Enigma machine he helped to protect convoys in the Atlantic and allowed Britain to receive the goods it needed to fight on.

It brought the end of Nazi-ism and helped keep at least half of Europe free. But even a hero such as this was persecuted for his private life.

His homosexuality led to arrest, chemical castration and, many believe, prompted his suicide.

So it is not as though the Governments have not always snooped into their population's lives, but the extent of this was particularly shocking in the Snowden stories.

We are not yet at the stage of totalitarianism such as under the Soviet Union or North Korea today.

But many fear that, using the cover of protecting their nations from terrorism, Governments are taking early, covert steps along the path.

After all, the elite need to protect themselves and their position. Or so many would argue.

But, to return to the accolades poured onto Snowden.

Another award from Germany, where he is considered a particular hero, was the IQ award from Mensa Germany.

However, controversy surrounded the Mensa organization, which is not an institution renowned for causing such.

Mensa Germany proposed Snowden, but the main management committee of Mensa worldwide opposed and tried to cancel the nomination.

This was against its rules. The feud grew until it was impossible to sustain the nomination. As a result, Mensa members decided to take action, and gave the award to an actor, Jonny Lee Miller, in protest at the dispute.

The actor had played Sherlock Holmes in a film, Elementary.

Another award that prompted controversy was the Norsk PEN Ossietzsky Prize, which Snowden won in 2016. Norway is a country known for staying politically on the fence.

Snowden wished to collect the trophy, and applied to Norway for safe passage. Their Government refused to grant it.

Having received such immense official recognition, another field in which Snowden is widely supported lies in the world of technology.

Snowden earns a considerable sum each year from participating in remote, teleconference engagements.

Some estimates put this at $200000 per annum. His message in many of these is that the NSA is seeking to 'set fire to the future of the internet' and that it is the duty of those with the skills to do so to ensure that this does not happen.

In order to maintain secrecy around his location, Snowden uses multiple routers on the Google Hangouts site when contributing to such conferences.

One of the biggest of these was the South by Southwest Interactive Technology conference, which took place in March 2014.

It was located in Austin Texan and had three and half thousand attendees.

The CIA worked hard, but unsuccessfully, to get Snowden's invitation rescinded.

Amongst the general public, the impact of media campaigns against Snowden seem to have had more effect than elsewhere in the world.

However, it must also be remembered that the States was, in the immediate post Snowden revelations, beginning its journey to appointing Donald Trump as President.

This is not a population likely to support a young tech nerd, or computer geek, who has released damaging stories about an institution claiming to protect them.

In Britain, where revelations about the actions of GCHQ have caused severe unrest in some quarters, the majority of people thought Snowden to be heroic.

Twice as many people felt that it was good that the secrets had come into the public domain, although admittedly a large percentage were sitting on the fence.

Only one in five people thought that the publications were in the wrong.

The figures were even higher in Canada, where two out of three people were in support of the whistleblower.

And in Germany, one in three people said that they would offer him refuge in their homes should the need arise.

He still has a majority support in the US. But opinion is mixed. Almost twice as many would call him a traitor as those who would say hero.

But most people sit on the fence. As time has progressed, these figures have stayed broadly the same.

Many of his supporters felt that to move to Russia was an unwise move. That there was still sufficient bad feeling towards the old enemy for the move to see Snowden labelled a traitor.

Even worse, a commie… which disregard the fact that Russia now operates an extremely capitalist economy. However, these fears are not particularly supported by the facts.

There is a slightly increased negative reaction towards Snowden, but it is not consistent across the questions asked in surveys.

For example, an increase in the numbers over time who thought it was wrong for him to leak were countered by an increase in the numbers who thought that it was wrong to prosecute him.

Perhaps unsurprisingly, his greatest support is amongst the young, whilst the over 65s were most against his actions.

But the revelations led to worsening feelings towards the US across the world. Not only was their antagonism towards the US monitoring, but a belief that it does not respect the freedoms of its own people.

Nonetheless, if Snowden was supported widely in the world, and narrowly in his homeland, officials in the US felt differently.

In an attempt to avoid public criticism, Federal prosecutors sought to charge Snowden in secret.

He was charged with two instances of breaking the Espionage Act and one of theft of Government property.

The secrecy lasted just a week, before the charges were exposed.

Each is interesting in its own way.

By pursuing the claim that the secrets were Government property the US administration was reinforcing its belief that it was within its rights to eavesdrop on its own people.

In addition, charges under the Espionage Act can lead to trial behind closed doors. He was specifically accused of unauthorized

communication of national defense
information.

The second charge was of willful
communication of intelligence information to
an unauthorized person.

President Obama invited Snowden to return
from exile to face the charges, but the
whistleblower believed that any proceedings
would take place in secret.

He felt it was typical of Obama to offer an
option for Snowden to make his case, when
that option would be entirely in the hands of
the prosecutors. He believed that such
duplicity *was possible* under the Obama regime.

In a move echoing GCHQ hijacking of other
legislation to give authority to its snooping,

the employment of the law contradicted its original purpose.

It had been established a century previously, and was designed to deal with spies during the First World War.

Many would say it is typical of Governments, in whatever country, to be as arrogant as to assume that the population would not see through such moves.

If the US authorities remained determined to pursue Snowden, then the European Parliament felt differently, albeit narrowly.

In 2015 they passed a resolution that EU states should drop any criminal charges they had issued against Snowden, and prevent any attempts to extradite him.

They declared that his status as a 'whistleblower and international human rights defender' needed to be recognized.

Although the resolution was non-binding, it pleased Snowden, who described it as a 'game changer', one that gave his cause a chance to move forward.

Other institutions within the United States were also firm in their reaction to Snowden's revelations.

Apparently, the US Army restricted access to the Guardian's website to its soldiers – this included any access to serving forces in Afghanistan, the Middle East and South Asia.

(Isn't it rumored that North Korea restricts its citizens access to the Internet?)

When the 100000 target of signatories to a petition seeking a pardon for Snowden was reached, the Government was obliged to respond.

It did not do so for nine months, and when it did, simply reported that Snowden must face the consequences of his actions.

The House Intelligence Committee wrote to Obama, urging him not to issue a pardon.

Others went further. James Woolsey, an ex-director of the CIA, said that Snowden should be executed if convicted of treason.

One of the reasons for such vehement official opposition to Snowden is the claim that his leaks put serving officers at risk.

Military intelligence claimed that most of the files he had copied related to military activity, and had encouraged terrorists to change their tactics.

This would, in many cases, negate possibly years of surveillance.

However, both Greenwald, and Snowden's attorney, Ben Wizner, refuted these claims.

During the First World War, British soldiers were sometimes executed, or shot at dawn, by their own side.

Their crimes were usually for cowardice, but most likely the victims were suffering from shell shock, a debilitating mental health disease.

However, it was known that the hierarchy felt that to execute a soldier would be a good deterrent to others from practicing 'cowardice.'

Despite enormous evidence regarding the soldiers' mental states, numerous requests for a pardon were denied. It took more than 90 years for them to be issued.

Another of the arguments used by the US for pursuing charges against Snowden employs a similar premise.

In some quarters, it is felt that should he be pardoned, that would open the gate for others to seek to expose unpalatable information.

In addition to pursuing charges, claims were made to undermine Snowden's credibility.

A former NSA director claimed that the former employee's actions were motivated by revenge, because he had not received the promotion he felt that he merited.

As we saw earlier, there is evidence to dispute this claim. However, some of the US political establishment are more supportive of Snowden's actions.

In 2014, the Republican party renounced the NSA's actions as:

'An invasion into the personal lives of American Citizens that violates the right of Free Speech.'

They believed that the NSA had breached both the First and the Fourth Amendments of the Constitution.

A former congressman, Ron Paul, sought to raise support for a clemency order to be given to Snowden.

Rather than acting 'narcissistically', as some opponents had claimed, Paul felt that the young man had sacrificed an enormous amount to bring to light a wrong doing.

And in 2014 former President Jimmy Carter indicated that he would, had he the power, entertain the thought that Snowden should be pardoned.

The former Vice President Al Gore took a more balanced line. Whilst recognizing that Snowden had broken the law, and that was wrong, he felt that what he exposed was even worse.

However, support from the establishment remains limited for Snowden.

In 2014, the Obama nominated Deputy Defense secretary Ashton Carter called the whistleblower a knuckle head, saying he was a 'cyber Pearl Harbour'.

The US media was also largely opposed to Snowden. In a report, the Washington Post said that he should still face trial.

Whilst the paper supported the view that the NSA phone hacking was unacceptable, many of Snowden's other revelations compromised legitimate security.

When it cited the example of the exposure of Prism, the journalistic community was forced to cry 'hypocrisy', as the paper had accepted a share of the Pullitzer prize.

For its reports of…the exposure of Prism.

Time to flee

With secrets that he knew would shock the world, and fearing reprisals from the US security agencies Snowden was becoming trapped.

His well-paid job, his girlfriend, his career was now on the line; and his personal fears were growing.

It was May 2013, and Snowden told his bosses that he had to leave Hawaii for the mainland. He suffered periodically from epilepsy, and told his employers that he was leaving for treatment.

Instead, he flew to Hong Kong. Arriving on May 20th, he booked into a hotel, the Mira. So great was his fear that he would be tracked, and caught, that he did not even let the maids in to clean his room.

It soon became filled with used clothing and old food containers. He went out little, and only when he needed to, quickly returning to his refuge.

Such is the life of a fugitive from the US authorities. Fearing that his Government would seek to extradite him, he contacted a Canadian human rights lawyer, who was based in Hong Kong.

Robert Tibbo became his legal adviser. Snowden sought to remain in Hong Kong as long as could, and released information on the Chinese internet protocol addresses that the NCA monitored.

He hoped that this would gain him some time and support from the Chinese, who were in overall charge of Hong Kong.

He further revealed that the US monitored Hong Kong text traffic. It was in the hotel that he held numerous meetings with the journalists led by Glenn Greenwald.

Tibbo arranged for him to move into a small apartment which was used by asylum seekers to the principality. He hoped that such a move might shield Snowden from the authorities.

Some debate then follows about what happened next. Russian media, and later President Putin, claimed that he met with Russian officials, and stayed in their Embassy.

Lawyers for Snowden denied this.

Within eighteen days of the publication of Snowden's findings, the US revoked his passport. Travel now for the fugitive could only be with the support of other nations.

Having now passed on all of the documents he had downloaded to journalists, he sought the next stage of maintaining freedom.

Again, confusion followed as diplomatic relations became strained.

The US claimed that Hong Kong knew that they both wished to arrest Snowden and had revoked his passport.

Meanwhile, the Hong Kong authorities stated that the US had not followed Hong Kong law, so there was no case for keeping Snowden.

The result was that Snowden, accompanied by a WikiLeaks representative, Sarah Harrison, left for Moscow on a commercial flight, using the Russian carrier Aeroflot.

By destroying or giving away all of the details he had downloaded, he felt that he could protect himself from pressure from the Russian authorities to share his information.

On landing in Moscow, further confusion followed. He had a ticket on to Cuba, from where, according to WikiLeaks, he would continue to Ecuador.

Julian Assange, the WikiLeaks head, had already spent many years in refuge from extradition at the Ecuadorian Embassy in London, so this must have been a strong option as a final destination.

However, decisions had to be changed in Russia. Although it was planned as just a transit stop, a part of a safe route to a new refuge, he could not move on.

Possibly, as Glenn Greenwald claimed, the US had sorted out their errors regarding his passport, and it was now definitely cancelled, so he could not fly internationally.

More likely, pressure was put on Cuba to stop his passage through this country. Whichever the case, Cuba would not accept him, even in transit, and he was forced to remain in Russia.

Snowden believed that this was a deliberate move on the part of the US authorities. With him in Russia, they could create a case that he had 'defected' to a traditional enemy.

The Washington Post claimed, however, that it was Russia that halted his progress, whilst the then Cuban leader, Fidel Castro, denied that his country would have refused him access.

Snowden was left in the transit area of the Russian airport for many days. Thirty-nine, in fact, not really the sort of treatment you offer to people welcomed in your country.

President Putin called him an 'unwanted Christmas gift' but said that, as no crime had been committed in Russia, he was free to move on.

With his passport now revoked, his only option was to remain in Russia and seek asylum there.

Initially, he was granted a one year stay, but the possibility of an extension was expressed.

Later in the year, his father visited him in Russia, and returned to say that he felt his son was safe there, and in the right place. By this stage, he also felt that his son would not receive a fair trial in the US.

Snowden possibly found a job in Russia, working for a large website. However, some doubt exists about this. The source was his Russian lawyer, and the Guardian at least did not trust the information.

Whilst he maintained that he had no information with him in Russia, British intelligence sources reported, or perhaps leaked, to the Times that Russian and

Chinese experts had cracked encryption codes.

This meant that British agents had been compromised, and had to be withdrawn from live operations.

Given the secrecy surrounding such information, no corroboration was available, and it could have been a part of the on-going plan to discredit Snowden.

Certainly, he claims that he had nothing with him in Moscow.

Reports coming out of Russia suggested that he was well, and the security services had not taken control of him.

Later in the year, he was invited to testify before the German Parliament in their investigation into the monitoring of their Chancellor, Angela Merkel.

Snowden agreed to do so, but asked to do it either in front of the US Congress, or in Berlin. He still claimed to be in Russia purely because the US had retracted his passport, and had sought refuge in a Latin American country.

In a side issue, that many Snowden supporters felt significant, the Presidential plane of the Bolivian leader, Evo Morales, was forced to land in Europe.

It was searched, and it believed that the US had been tipped off that Snowden was on board.

Snowden also attempted to gain asylum to Brazil, offering to support its investigation into spying by the US into its president, Dilma Rousseff.

Later, US officials tried to spread the story that Snowden had in fact been supported by Russian experts all along.

As Snowden's temporary asylum expired, he was given a three-year residency permit. This empowers him to travel abroad for up to three months at a time, and move freely in the country.

However, it does not give him permanent asylum.

Other secrets

We have looked in some detail at four of the revelations Snowden revealed – the collection of phone data, Prism, monitoring of world leaders and the cracking of internet encryption.

But these were just the very small tip of an extremely large iceberg. What else did Snowden discover and, through his journalist contacts, share with the world?

Anybody with their mobile phone switched on and flying above 10000 feet was considered fair game.

Their signal could be tracked and their location identified. A simple cross check would then list the flight, the passengers on it and then the user could be identified.

The British were very much at the forefront in this technology.

A particular target for both the US and the British was Air France, but, as technology improved since the mid noughties [~~noughties~~ *nineties*], more and more carriers permitted the use of mobiles on board.

A wider issue that many will consider even more alarming is the NSA's development and use of malware to infect computers across the world.

As worrying, the NSA's own security was weak enough to allow hackers to break in and steal it. A group called ShadowBrokers auctioned the malware they had acquired for personal profit.

The malware, definitely originating from the NSA since the identification codes provided by ShadowBrokers were exactly the same as those in a Snowden paper, could be used to target anyone.

That included foreign governments, terrorist organizations, or a child playing an online game. In fact, one is left with a slight feeling that the NSA designers live in a world where the seriousness of their work is not fully clear to them.

The names chosen for their invasive programmes include Eligible Bombshell, Polarsneeze and Seconddate.

These names imply a group of people living so far out of reality that they have no real concept of the potential harm they are causing. The names suggest no more than a childish game.

* Seconddate intercepts requests to the web and redirects computers to an NSA web server, where they are infected with malware.

* Seconddate is just one part of a much larger infiltration programme called Baddecision – yes, genuinely. It really beggars belief that such ironic names could be employed for so serious purposes.

Although innocent people were caught up by this programme, the name implies that they are justifiable victims.

* Baddecision tricks the user into believing that they are on a safe website, whereas they

have been directed to an NSA site where their computer is infected.

Documentation from Snowden shows how the NSA could use the software to make a behind the scenes attack on a user visiting an utterly legitimate website.

In the leak, the CNN is referenced as an example. The paper goes on to say that in this scenario, the user's computer becomes, wait for it, 'whacked!'

Snowden's inside knowledge of how the NSA works identified that the hack by cyber criminals could have been caused by a very simple mistake at the security agency.

He explains how agents are told never to leave behind any traces on a server they have infiltrated. But, as he says, people 'get lazy'.

It is possible that hackers found the programmes hiding on a normal server, rather than one run by the NSA.

So it seems that the reason for the successful hack is either lack of care in employees' actions, or inadequacy in security systems. A pleasant choice.

Some of the papers downloaded by Snowden offered an insight into the people working at the NSA.

We have already seen that the names they gave to highly serious plans which could cause substantial harm and intrusion to ordinary people were dismissive and lacking in gravitas.

Their jokey irony suggests a disregard for the interests, privacy and lives of others.

However, one journalist was able to use the Snowden leaks to talk to an ex NSA hacker, to learn more.

Peter Maass writes for the Intercept, a magazine co-founded by Glenn Greenwald which comments on issues connected to civil liberties and justice.

He had spoken to official NSA sources, but they had, unsurprisingly, offered little insight into the agency's activities.

He had discovered, through the Snowden papers, details of some NSA employees, but not enough to get a real insight.

Although the advice columnist who created the zany 'Ask Zelda' articles was strangely alarming.

But when Maass employed the Snowden sources and met a pitbull owning, heavy metal loving ex NSA hacker, the former employee was happy to talk.

He was an outspoken man, who had been active on social media.

Hackers do, pardoning the generalization, tend to be anti-authoritarian people who hold little respect for social norms or laws – after all, their actions are to invade the privacy of others.

But many, possibly the majority, of top level hackers do hold down serious jobs, mostly with Government agencies.

The department of justice has skillfully manipulated this situation into place. Firstly, it made hacking a dangerous activity, with prison a very serious possibility for those caught.

We know how seriously the US takes this. When an autistic teenager hacked the Pentagon from his bedroom in England, the authorities might have sought him out to learn how he did it.

Hopefully that would stop anybody more malicious from repeating the act. But no, they launched a long extradition process to try to get the hacker to the US, where he would face trial and a long prison sentence.

This for a quite severely disabled child.

Having established a situation where hacking in the States is a dangerous past time (a fair enough situation, most would agree) it then sought to give a legitimate outlet to these people.

Jobs with the authorities. This included the NSA, army, agencies employed by the security services and military, and many more.

The NSA was a desirable employer for the best hackers, because it was an intellectually stimulating environment, with the brightest people and the best resources.

The hacker to whom Maass spoke, he called him Lamb (after a heavy metal group) had progressed in the NSA through self-teaching and a willingness to talk to others.

But one of the great ethical dilemmas quickly arose in the discussions with Lamb. He was prepared to hack into systems administrators – innocent people – to access his end targets, in this case terrorists.

And the hacking of the middle men meant invading every bit of their technological lives, including email and social media.

And this hacking was not being done by elected people with a long history of empathy towards the public.

No, it was being done by the kind of people who call their annual conference Def Con, and who seem to hold the general public in disregard.

A leak from Snowden had shown some of Lamb's work. A hand drawn diagram demonstrating how an entire country's internet traffic could be redirected to the NSA contained cartoon drawings and dismissive, jokey comments.

As well as the admission that they would use their access to everything to locate the bad guys they sought.

Lamb's attitude, which might reasonably be seen as typical of the NSA hackers, was that if people failed to protect themselves online, then it was their fault if they were attacked.

A case of the blame laying at the victim's door.

The iceberg of Snowden's revelations is still floating deeply beneath the waters of this book, but we will look at one more chunk.

This relates to the UK's activities. A fear was growing at the security agency, MI5, that GCHQ was mopping up more information than it could cope with.

By accessing information from so many sources, and at such levels of intensity, clues were slipping through the net, and that was leading to mistakes.

Indeed, a while after this report, the soldier Lee Rigby was murdered in broad daylight. His attackers, who also attempted to decapitate him, turned out to be known to the British security services.

But the seriousness of the threat they presented had been lost amongst the deluge of information the services kept.

The situation was made worse when the Government passed the Investigatory Powers Bill which gave more authority for agents to access data.

Although the bill was passed – there are more votes in stopping terrorism than protecting individuals, it seems – much angst was caused.

It seemed to many that the bill would not help the identification of terrorists, indeed would hinder it. The additional data about ordinary people would obscure the information security agencies needed.

An example was the service code named Preston. This is meant to be used to intercept data from known targets, who have been certified as a threat by a Government minister.

Yet, with more than five million communications – email, internet, phone, text etc. – in one six-month period only 3% had been reviewed.

This from a programme which specifically targets known threats.

But Snowden's revelations revealed more. GCHQ was not asking for more powers, it felt it had authority in any case to do pretty much as it wished.

The problem was that agencies such as the police, the tax office and suchlike wanted to make use of the troves of data gathered.

But, since 'terrorism' could not be a hedge used to hide behind for the tax man, a stop gap had to be put in place until the climate was right for a proper, population disturbing, bill could pass through parliament.

Milkwhite was the name of that stopgap. This allowed domestic agencies to trawl through the GCHQ data to find information of interest.

This meant that data spied upon on the premise of stopping domestic threats and terrorists, was now being used to identify breaches in tax law.

And even if that was seen as acceptable, it was only by the study of millions other pieces of completely innocent data that this information could be found.

We would not have known this, been able to hold our political masters to account over it, had it not been for Edward Snowden.

What next?

On the website, edwardsnowden.com, Snowden succinctly outlines his motivations for the acts he committed.

He says: 'I can't in good conscience allow the US government to destroy privacy, internet freedom and basic liberties for people around the world with this massive surveillance machine they're secretly building.'

It was for protection of the internet, and the privacy of people that Snowden gave up his job, his home, the country of his birth. He lost regular contact with his parents, friends and girlfriend.

He is indicted under three charges, two of which date back to world war 1. The internet was not so big back then, relying on pigeons instead of email.

Several countries in the world have been issued with arrest and extradition orders for the whistleblower, and even received threats to reduce trade should they offer asylum.

People associated with Snowden have been hassled and questioned.

Whistleblowers do not have a record of good treatment by the US. Chelsea Manning was sentenced to 35 years in prison.

Obama proudly claimed to have prosecuted twice as many people as any previous administration under the Espionage Act.

We can only speculate whether Trump would see that as shameful, or a legitimate target to beat.

At the outset of the publication of his revelations, Snowden made (largely through WikiLeaks) 28 asylum applications to 27 countries (Russia featured twice).

His stay in Russian may come to an end in the Summer of 2017.

Given that his location is kept highly secret, it may be that he has already left.

It is hard to say what will happen next. It could well be the case that Russia extends its welcoming hand. Relations with the US have been disrupted by accusations of interference in the Presidential election.

Equally, Putin and Trump seem to get on well, and Trump may see it as a propaganda scoop if he can persuade Russia to extradite the wanted man.

Other countries would offer asylum to Snowden, particularly in Latin America. However, two problems exist here. Firstly, getting there.

He has no valid passport (at least, as far as we know). Therefore, any travel would need to be surreptitious. This is not an insurmountable problem.

More serious is that Governments change. Pressure could be placed on a country to release Snowden for extradition, with the US offering incentives for this to happen.

Whatever the support offered by a current leader, a future incumbent could see things differently.

Wherever Snowden ends up, he will know, however, that he has many supporters around the world.

But also, a good many detractors.

Conclusion – A Kind Of Legacy

Edward Snowden's decision to reveal the practices of the NSA and its intrusion into the lives of ordinary people has created an interesting legacy.

In May 2014, the House Judiciary Committee made recommendations to limit the NSA's actions.

Although the recommendations see sawed for over a year, some changes to limit its activities were eventually approved.

Funding was also cut to some of its programmes.

Regarding the constitution, suits have been filed that are drawing the Supreme Court to a decision as to the extent the fourth amendment has been breached by the wide seizure of data.

Several investigations have taken place into surveillance procedures, although at the time of writing no concrete changes had been made.

So, at the legislative level, in the US, progress has been slow.

But at the wider popular level, awareness of the NSA's activities created unrest, and distrust.

Perhaps, and this is just a deduction, it was the beginning of the process of distrust of establishment figures that led to Donald Trump being elected to the White House.

If this is the case, and Trump recognizes it as so, that could be good news for Snowden.

Further afield, there were numerous international ramifications from Snowden's revelations.

Whilst Britain has done little in real terms, the European Parliament Civil liberties committee investigated fully.

Germany was especially outraged by the NSA activities. However, its inquiry identified that some of its own surveillance systems were, without parliamentary permission, passing on information about German citizens.

Prosecution has been threatened should this continue.

Investigations have taken place in Australia, Brazil – even the United Nations.

But perhaps Snowden's greatest legacy is that people now know what their Governments are doing to them.

At least they can form their own opinions on the wrongness or otherwise of their own leaders gathering information about their own citizens.

No longer is it happening in absolute secrecy.

Made in the USA
Middletown, DE
27 September 2019